Per i nonni
Mario e Luisa

British Library Cataloguing in Publication Data
McKee, David
   Who's a clever baby then?
   I. Title
   823'.914 [J]   PZ7
   ISBN 0-86264-201-9

© 1988 by David McKee
First published in Great Britain in 1988 by Andersen Press Ltd., 62–65 Chandos Place, London WC2. Published in
Australia by Century Hutchinson Australia Pty. Ltd., 16–22 Church Street, Hawthorn, Victoria 3122.
All rights reserved. Colour separated by Photolitho AG Offsetreproduktionen, Gossau, Zürich, Switzerland. Printed in
Italy by Grafiche AZ, Verona.

10 9 8 7 6 5 4 3 2 1

Who's a Clever Baby then?

David McKee

Andersen Press · London
Hutchinson · Australia

"Who's a clever baby then?" said Grandma. "And where's my oofum boofum pussy cat? Say 'cat', Baby."

"Dog," said Baby.

"Oh Baby, look at the tiger, just look at the tiger," said Grandma. "Oh what terrible teeth has Trevor the television tiger. Say 'tiger', Baby."

"Dog," said Baby.

"Oh come on, Baby," said Grandma. "Let's feed Freddy, the funny fat freckled fish. Say 'fish', Baby."

"Dog," said Baby.

"Oh Baby, look there," said Grandma. "See the birds? The big brown birds biting Beryl's beautiful blue berries. Say 'bird', Baby."

"Dog," said Baby.

"Oh my. Oh my. Look at the teddies, Baby," said Grandma. "There are fat teddies and tall teddies, thin teddies and small teddies, young teddies and old teddies, curly teddies and bald teddies. Pink teddies and blue teddies, and some bigger-than-you teddies. Say 'teddy', Baby."

"Dog," said Baby.

"Oh Baby," said Grandma. "There's Peter and Pamela Pointer packing a perfect painting of a pretty pink paddling penguin. Say 'penguin', Baby."

"Dog," said Baby.

"Oh Baby," said Grandma. "See the statue? See strong Samson silently struggling with Simon, the serious stone lion. Say 'lion', Baby."

"Dog," said Baby.

"Oh ho. Oh ho, Baby," said Grandma. "There's another baby, Baby. A lovely wovely baby, Baby, an oochy coochy baby, Baby. And where's my clever wever baby, Baby? Say 'baby', Baby."

"Dog," said Baby.

"Up Baby, down Baby, to Baby and fro Baby. Rumpity rumpity rumpity rump," said Grandma. "Does the clever baby like Edward, the enormous electric elephant, then? Say 'elephant', Baby."

"Dog," said Baby.

"Oh, hey, Baby," said Grandma. "Look at the clockwork crocodile. It's a cheerful crocodile, a creeping crocodile, a clicking crocodile, a crazy crimson-coloured crocodile. Say 'crocodile', Baby."

"Dog," said Baby.

"Oh ha ha ha," laughed Grandma. "Oh ha ha ha. Oh look, Baby. Ha ha ha, look at the horse, Baby. Oh he he he. Oh what a comical clowning circus horse. Oh ho ho ho. Oh what a handsome happy humorous horse. Oh ha ha ha. Say 'horse', Baby."

"Dog," said Baby.

"Oh Baby, who's a clever baby then?" said Grandma. "Look, my clever baby, there's a big booful wooful doggie woggie for my clever wever baby. Such a darling dog, Baby. Who's a clever baby then? Say 'dog', Baby."

"Cat," said Baby.